foreword

A small book full of truffles and toffee, barks and brittle, fudge and fruit bites—for someone with a sweet tooth, this is heaven! Dip into these pages to find miniature delights: colourful Cream Cheese Mints to fill a teacher's gift mug; Chocolate Crunch to thank a special babysitter; Cashew Pecan Praline for the staff party.

At Company's Coming, we know how much fun it is to put together a tray of tiny treats, and we've compiled some of the best from our cookbooks. Many of these can be made ahead for last-minute gifts (add a copy of this book for the candy cravers on your list!). And with plenty on hand, you'll always be well-stocked when you have drop-in guests or an urge to indulge. Now that's what makes for sweet dreams!

Jean Paré

chocolate pralines

A plate or box of these candies makes a wonderful thank-you gift!

Brown sugar, packed	1 1/2 cups	375 mL
Granulated sugar	1 1/2 cups	375 mL
Evaporated milk (or half-and-half cream)	1 cup	250 mL
Salt	1/2 tsp.	2 mL
Chopped pecans	2 cups	500 mL
Unsweetened chocolate baking squares (1 oz., 28 g, each), chopped	2	2
Hard margarine (or butter)	2 tbsp.	30 mL
Vanilla extract	1 tsp.	5 mL

Combine first 4 ingredients in large heavy saucepan. Heat and stir on medium until boiling. Boil for about 5 minutes, stirring constantly, until mixture reaches soft ball stage (234° to 240°F, 112° to 116°C) on candy thermometer (see Tip, page 64) or until small amount dropped into very cold water forms a soft ball that flattens on its own accord when removed. Remove from heat.

Add remaining 4 ingredients. Stir until slightly thickened. Quickly drop, using about 2 tsp. (10 mL) for each, onto waxed paper. If mixture becomes too thick to drop, reheat slightly. Makes about 36 pralines.

1 praline: 140 Calories; 6.8 g Total Fat (3.8 g Mono, 1.2 g Poly, 1.4 g Sat); 2 mg Cholesterol; 21 g Carbohydrate; 1 g Fibre; 1 g Protein; 56 mg Sodium

chocolate brittle

Made in the microwave, this recipe is a snap to put together!

Granulated sugar	1 cup	250 mL
White corn syrup	1/2 cup	125 mL
Dry-roasted peanuts	1 cup	250 mL
Hard margarine (or butter)	2 tbsp.	30 mL
Vanilla extract	1 tsp.	5 mL
Baking soda	1 1/2 tsp.	7 mL
TOPPING		
Semi-sweet chocolate chips	3/4 cup	175 mL
Chopped unsalted peanuts	1/3 cup	75 mL

Combine sugar and corn syrup in ungreased 2 quart (2 L) microwave-safe casserole. Microwave, uncovered, on high (100%) for about 4 minutes until sugar is dissolved and mixture is bubbling.

Add peanuts. Stir. Microwave, uncovered, on high (100%) for about 6 minutes, checking at 1 minute intervals, until golden.

Add margarine and vanilla. Stir. Microwave, uncovered, on high (100%) for 1 minute. Stir.

Add baking soda. Stir. Mixture will foam. Immediately pour onto greased baking sheet with sides. Spread evenly into thin layer.

Topping: Sprinkle chocolate chips on hot peanut mixture. Let stand until chocolate chips are softened. Spread evenly. Sprinkle with peanuts. Chill until set. Break brittle into irregular-shaped pieces, about 1 1/2 x 2 inches (3.8 x 5 cm) each. Makes about 30 pieces.

***1 piece:** 114 Calories; 5.5 g Total Fat (2.6 g Mono, 1.2 g Poly, 1.4 g Sat); 0 mg Cholesterol; 16 g Carbohydrate; 1 g Fibre; 2 g Protein; 120 mg Sodium*

four-seed brittle

Who says sweets are bad for you? These seeds are full of healthy nutrients.
Perfect for a lunch-bag treat.

Butter (or hard margarine), softened	1/4 cup	60 mL
Brown sugar, packed	1/2 cup	125 mL
Golden corn syrup	1/3 cup	75 mL
All-purpose flour	1/2 cup	125 mL
Raw pumpkin seeds	1/4 cup	60 mL
Unsalted, roasted sunflower seeds	1/4 cup	60 mL
Flaxseed	2 tbsp.	30 mL
Sesame seeds, toasted (see Tip, page 64)	2 tbsp.	30 mL

Cream butter and brown sugar in medium bowl. Add corn syrup. Beat well. Add flour. Mix well.

Add remaining 4 ingredients. Mix well. Roll out evenly between 2 sheets of parchment (not waxed) paper to 11 x 17 inch (28 x 43 cm) rectangle. Transfer parchment paper with seed mixture to 11 x 17 inch (28 x 43 cm) baking sheet with sides. Chill for 10 minutes. Discard top sheet of parchment paper. Bake in 400°F (205°C) oven for 5 to 10 minutes until golden. Let stand on baking sheet for 10 minutes. Remove parchment paper with seed mixture from baking sheet and place on wire rack to cool. Break brittle into irregular-shaped pieces, about 2 x 2 inches (5 x 5 cm) each. Makes about 40 pieces.

1 piece: 51 Calories; 2.5 g Total Fat (0.7 g Mono, 0.8 g Poly, 0.9 g Sat); 3 mg Cholesterol; 7 g Carbohydrate; trace Fibre; 1 g Protein; 18 mg Sodium

cashew pecan praline

Store this attractive candy in an airtight container for up to eight weeks. When processed to a fine powder, praline is wonderful sprinkled on a frosted cake, ice cream or pudding.

Pecan halves	1 1/2 cups	375 mL
Raw cashews	1 1/2 cups	375 mL
Granulated sugar	3 cups	750 mL
Water	3/4 cup	175 mL

Spread pecans and cashews evenly in ungreased shallow pan. Bake in 350°F (175°C) oven for 5 to 10 minutes, stirring or shaking often, until just toasted. Turn oven off. Let stand in pan in oven to keep warm.

Combine sugar and water in medium heavy saucepan. Heat and stir on medium-high for about 5 minutes until boiling and sugar is dissolved. Boil, uncovered, for about 10 minutes, without stirring, brushing side of saucepan with wet pastry brush to dissolve any sugar crystals, until golden. Remove from heat. Add nuts. Stir. Immediately pour into greased 10 x 15 inch (25 x 38 cm) jelly roll pan. Working quickly, spread mixture evenly to sides of pan. Let stand in jelly roll pan on wire rack for 1 to 2 hours until cooled. Break praline into irregular-shaped pieces, about 1 1/2 x 4 inches (3.8 x 10 cm) each. Makes about 24 pieces.

1 piece: 202 Calories; 9 g Total Fat (5.5 g Mono, 1.9 g Poly, 1.2 g Sat); 0 mg Cholesterol; 31 g Carbohydrate; 1 g Fibre; 2 g Protein; 2 mg Sodium

sweet sesame snack

Great nibblies for hiking, relaxing on the deck or watching the game. For larger pieces, pack the warm mixture into a 9 x 13 inch (22 x 33 cm) pan lined with waxed paper. Once it's cooled, break it into bite-sized pieces.

Large flake rolled oats	2 cups	500 mL
Medium unsweetened coconut	1/2 cup	125 mL
Sesame seeds	1/2 cup	125 mL
Sliced almonds, coarsely chopped	1/3 cup	75 mL
Brown sugar, packed	1/3 cup	75 mL
Cooking oil	1/4 cup	60 mL
Golden corn syrup	1/4 cup	60 mL
Liquid honey	1/4 cup	60 mL
Water	1/4 cup	60 mL
Vanilla extract	1 1/2 tsp.	7 mL
Salt	1/4 tsp.	1 mL

Combine first 4 ingredients in 2 quart (2 L) microwave-safe shallow baking dish.

Combine remaining 7 ingredients in medium microwave-safe bowl. Microwave, uncovered, on high (100%) for about 4 minutes until brown sugar is dissolved and mixture is bubbling. Pour over oat mixture. Stir until coated. Microwave, uncovered, on high (100%) for 4 minutes. Stir. Microwave, uncovered, on high (100%) for 6 to 7 minutes, stirring every 2 minutes, until toasted. Spread loosely on large waxed paper-lined baking sheet to cool. Makes about 5 cups (1.25 L).

1/2 cup (125 mL): 319 Calories; 16.5 g Total Fat (6.9 g Mono, 4.6 g Poly, 4.1 g Sat); 0 mg Cholesterol; 40 g Carbohydrate; 3 g Fibre; 6 g Protein; 79 mg Sodium

candied peanuts and dates

These triangles satisfy a variety of cravings—they're sweet, chewy, crunchy and chocolatey. Cut the candied mixture into squares first, and then slice in half diagonally to create triangles.

Butter (or hard margarine)	6 tbsp.	100 mL
Brown sugar, packed	3 tbsp.	50 mL
Corn syrup	2 tbsp.	30 mL
Unsalted peanuts	1 cup	250 mL
Finely chopped pitted dates	1/2 cup	125 mL
Box of candy-coated chocolates	2 oz.	56 g

Heat first 3 ingredients in large heavy saucepan on medium, stirring occasionally, until brown sugar is dissolved and mixture is bubbling.

Add peanuts and dates. Heat and stir for about 3 minutes until peanuts are coated and mixture is slightly thickened. Remove from heat. Let stand for 15 minutes. If mixture gets too cool, it will be difficult to mix in candies.

Add candies. Mix well. Line 8 x 8 inch (20 x 20 cm) pan with foil, leaving 1 inch (2.5 cm) overhang on 2 sides. Grease foil with cooking spray. Press peanut mixture evenly in prepared pan. Cool completely. Holding foil, remove candied mixture from pan. Discard foil. Cuts into 24 triangles.

1 triangle: 97 Calories; 6.7 g Total Fat (2.4 g Mono, 1.1 g Poly, 2.3 g Sat); 8.2 mg Cholesterol; 9 g Carbohydrate; 1 g Fibre; 2 g Protein; 34 mg Sodium

spiced toffee nuts

A deliciously spiced mix of nuts in a crunchy toffee coating, this tempting treat won't stay around for long.

Egg white (large)	1	1
Hazelnuts (filberts), toasted (see Tip, page 64)	1 cup	250 mL
Pecan halves, toasted (see Tip, page 64)	1 cup	250 mL
Whole natural almonds, toasted (see Tip, page 64)	1 cup	250 mL
Granulated sugar	2/3 cup	150 mL
Liquid honey	1/2 cup	125 mL
Ground cinnamon	1 tsp.	5 mL
Ground ginger	1 tsp.	5 mL
Ground nutmeg	1 tsp.	5 mL
Salt	3/4 tsp.	4 mL

Beat egg white in medium bowl until frothy.

Add remaining 9 ingredients. Mix well. Spread on greased baking sheet with sides. Bake in 350°F (175°C) oven for about 20 minutes, stirring often, until golden. Spread nuts in single layer to cool. Break into bite-sized pieces. Makes about 3 1/3 cups (825 mL).

1/3 cup (75 mL): 375 Calories; 24.2 g Total Fat (16.7 g Mono, 4.4 g Poly, 2.1 g Sat); 0 mg Cholesterol; 40 g Carbohydrate; 4 g Fibre; 6 g Protein; 187 mg Sodium

chocolate crunch

Plan to make lots! Even if you hide this crunch, it's sure to be found. Drizzle any leftover melted chocolate into the shape of your sweetie's initial for a fast surprise!

Smooth peanut butter	1/2 cup	125 mL
Dark corn syrup	1/4 cup	60 mL
Crisp rice cereal	1/2 cup	125 mL
Semi-sweet chocolate baking squares (1 oz., 28 g, each), chopped	4	4

Combine peanut butter and corn syrup in small bowl. Add cereal. Mix well. Roll into 8 inch (20 cm) long log. Chill. Cut with sharp knife into 1/4 inch (6 mm) slices.

Heat chocolate in small heavy saucepan on lowest heat, stirring often, until almost melted. Do not overheat. Remove from heat. Stir until smooth. Place 1 slice on fork. Dip into chocolate until coated, allowing excess to drip back into pan. Place on waxed paper. Repeat with remaining slices and chocolate. Let stand until set. Makes about 32 pieces.

1 piece: 52 Calories; 3.4 g Total Fat 1.4 g Mono, 0.6 g Poly, 1.1 g Sat); 0 mg Cholesterol; 5 g Carbohydrate; trace Fibre; 1 g Protein; 25 mg Sodium

almond fruit bark

You can make this colourful bark in November and freeze for up to a month.
Packed in a decorative Christmas tin, this bark makes a delicious gift.

Dark (or white) chocolate bars (3 1/2 oz., 100 g, each), chopped	4	4
Dried cherries	1/2 cup	125 mL
Whole natural almonds, toasted (see Tip, page 64)	1/2 cup	125 mL
Chopped dried apricot	1/3 cup	75 mL

Heat chocolate in medium heavy saucepan on lowest heat, stirring often, until almost melted. Do not overheat. Remove from heat. Stir until smooth.

Add remaining 3 ingredients. Mix well. Spread evenly on waxed paper-lined baking sheet with sides. Chill for about 30 minutes until set. Remove from pan. Break bark into irregular-shaped pieces, about 1 1/2 x 4 inches (3.8 x 10 cm) each. Makes about 24 pieces.

1 piece: 112 Calories; 6.8 g Total Fat (2.8 g Mono, 0.5 g Poly, 3.1 g Sat); 0 mg Cholesterol; 14 g Carbohydrate; 1 g Fibre; 2 g Protein; 2 mg Sodium

dalmatian bark

A two-ingredient treat that's all bark for lots of bites! Kids will love adding the "spots" to the white chocolate.

White chocolate bars (3 1/2 oz., 100 g, each), chopped	5	5
Semi-sweet chocolate chips	1/2 cup	125 mL

Line 9 x 13 inch (22 x 33 cm) pan with waxed paper, leaving 1 inch (2.5 cm) overhang on long sides. Heat white chocolate in medium heavy saucepan on lowest heat, stirring often, until almost melted. Do not overheat. Remove from heat. Stir until smooth. Spread evenly in prepared pan.

Sprinkle with chocolate chips, creating an uneven pattern like a Dalmatian's spots. Gently tap pan on work surface to settle chips into chocolate. Chill for about 2 hours until set. Holding waxed paper, remove bark from pan. Discard waxed paper. Break bark into irregular-shaped pieces, about 1 1/2 x 4 inches (3.8 x 10 cm) each. Makes about 18 pieces.

1 piece: 172 Calories; 9.9 g Total Fat (3.2 g Mono, 0.3 g Poly, 5.8 g Sat); 6 mg Cholesterol; 20 g Carbohydrate; trace Fibre; 2 g Protein; 25 mg Sodium

chocolate-coated mint patties

Use dark or milk chocolate wafers, depending on your taste.

Milk	6 tbsp.	100 mL
All-purpose flour	3 1/2 tbsp.	57 mL
Icing (confectioner's) sugar	3 cups	750 mL
Peppermint extract	3/4 tsp.	4 mL
Chocolate melting wafers (about 9 oz., 255 g)	1 1/3 cups	325 mL

Whisk milk into flour in small saucepan until smooth. Heat and stir on medium until boiling and thickened. Remove from heat.

Add icing sugar and extract. Mix well. Let stand for 5 minutes. Turn out onto icing sugar-coated surface. Knead for about 1 minute until smooth, adding more icing sugar if dough is sticky. Divide dough into 2 equal portions. Roll out each portion on icing sugar-coated surface into 1 inch (2.5 cm) diameter logs. Wrap logs with plastic wrap. Let stand at room temperature for at least 6 hours or overnight. Cut logs into 1/4 inch (6 mm) slices, re-shaping as necessary. Place on ungreased baking sheets. Let stand, uncovered, for about 1 hour, turning at halftime, until dry.

Heat chocolate wafers in small heavy saucepan on lowest heat, stirring often, until almost melted. Do not overheat. Remove from heat. Stir until smooth. Place 1 patty on fork. Dip into chocolate until coated, allowing excess to drip back into pan. Place on waxed paper. Make small swirl on top with spoon while chocolate is still soft. Repeat with remaining patties and chocolate. Let stand until set. Makes about 60 mint patties.

1 mint patty: 49 Calories; 1.3 g Total Fat (0.4 g Mono, 0.1 g Poly, 0.8 g Sat); 1 mg Cholesterol; 9 g Carbohydrate; trace Fibre; trace Protein; 4 mg Sodium

after-dinner mints

Store these snow-white, melt-in-your-mouth candies in an airtight container. For some variation, you can knead a drop of food colouring into a portion of dough.

Envelopes of unflavoured gelatin (1/4 oz., 7 g, each), about 3 tbsp., 50 mL	3	3
Water	1/2 cup	125 mL
Icing (confectioner's) sugar	2 cups	500 mL
Peppermint extract	1 1/2 tsp.	7 mL
Baking powder	1/4 tsp.	1 mL
Icing (confectioner's) sugar	4 cups	1 L

Sprinkle gelatin over water in medium saucepan. Let stand for 1 minute. Heat and stir on low until gelatin is dissolved. Remove from heat.

Add next 3 ingredients. Stir well.

Add second amount of icing sugar. Stir. Mixture will be sticky. Turn out onto icing sugar-coated surface. Knead for about 1 minute until smooth. Divide dough into 4 equal portions. Cover 3 portions with plastic wrap to prevent drying. Roll out 1 portion into 1/2 inch (12 mm) diameter rope. Cut into 1/2 inch (12 mm) pieces with scissors or knife. Arrange in single layer on waxed paper. Repeat with remaining portions. Let stand for about 1 hour until firm. Makes about 168 mints.

1 mint: 18 Calories; 0 g Total Fat (0 g Mono, 0 g Poly, 0 g Sat); 0 mg Cholesterol; 5 g Carbohydrate; 0 g Fibre; 0 g Protein; 1 mg Sodium

cream cheese mints

Kids love making this candy. You can add a few more drops of peppermint if you prefer your mints on the strong side. Refrigerate these in an airtight container.

Cream cheese, softened	4 oz.	125 g
Icing (confectioner's) sugar	3 1/2 cups	875 mL
Peppermint extract	1/8 tsp.	0.5 mL
Drop of green liquid food colouring	1	1
Drop of red liquid food colouring	1	1
Drop of yellow liquid food colouring	1	1
Granulated sugar	3/4 cup	175 mL

Mash cream cheese with fork in large bowl. Add icing sugar and extract. Mix well. Divide into 4 equal portions.

Place 1 portion in small bowl. Knead green food colouring into cream cheese mixture until colour is even (see Tip, page 64), adding more icing sugar if dough is sticky. Repeat with remaining dough and food colouring in separate bowls, leaving 1 portion white. Roll dough into 1/2 inch (12 mm) balls.

Roll balls in granulated sugar in small shallow dish until coated. Flatten balls with fork, thumb or bottom of glass. Place mints on waxed paper-lined baking sheet with sides. Let stand until dry. Chill. Makes about 146 mints.

1 mint: 19 Calories; 0.3 g Total Fat (0.1 g Mono, trace Poly, 0.2 g Sat); 1 mg Cholesterol; 4 g Carbohydrate; 0 g Fibre; trace Protein; 3 mg Sodium

fudgey chocolate mints

For a different presentation, drop these by the teaspoonful onto waxed paper. Let stand until set. If the chocolate mixture becomes too hard to drop, reheat on low until desired consistency.

Semi-sweet chocolate chips	2 cups	500 mL
Can of sweetened condensed milk	11 oz.	300 mL
Milk chocolate chips	1 cup	250 mL
Hard margarine (or butter)	2 tbsp.	30 mL
Vanilla extract	1 tsp.	5 mL
Peppermint extract	1/8 tsp.	0.5 mL

Combine all 6 ingredients in large heavy saucepan. Heat on medium-low, stirring often, until chocolate is melted and mixture is smooth. Line 9 x 9 inch (22 x 22 cm) pan with foil, leaving 1 inch (2.5 cm) overhang on 2 sides. Grease foil with cooking spray. Spread chocolate mixture evenly in prepared pan. Let stand until set. Holding foil, remove chocolate mixture from pan. Discard foil. Cut into 12 rows lengthwise and crosswise. Makes 144 mints.

1 mint: 28 Calories; 1.5 g Total Fat (0.5 g Mono, 0.1 g Poly, 0.9 g Sat); 1 mg Cholesterol; 4 g Carbohydrate; trace Fibre; 0 g Protein; 7 mg Sodium

nutty pecan logs

This impressive homemade candy has a nougat centre coated with caramel and nuts. You can wrap these logs in plastic wrap and store in an airtight container for four weeks, or freeze for longer storage.

Jar of marshmallow creme	7 oz.	198 g
Vanilla extract	1 tsp.	5 mL
Almond extract	1/4 tsp.	1 mL
Icing (confectioner's) sugar	3 cups	750 mL
COATING		
Bag of caramels (about 40)	12 oz.	340 g
Water	2 tbsp.	30 mL
Finely chopped pecans	1 1/2 cups	375 mL

Combine first 3 ingredients in large bowl.

Add icing sugar, 1 cup (250 mL) at a time, until sugar is absorbed and mixture is very thick and firm. Divide into 6 equal portions. Roll out each portion into 1 inch (2.5 cm) diameter logs. Place on ungreased baking sheet with sides. Chill in freezer for 15 minutes.

Coating: Combine caramels and water in medium heavy saucepan. Heat on medium-low, stirring often, until smooth. Roll each log in caramel mixture until coated.

Immediately roll each log in pecans in medium shallow dish until coated. Cut each log into 10 slices. Makes 60 slices.

1 slice: 74 Calories; 2.5 g Total Fat (1.4 g Mono, 0.5 g Poly, 0.5 g Sat); trace Cholesterol; 13 g Carbohydrate; trace Fibre; 1 g Protein; 13 mg Sodium

rum-and-butter balls

A delightfully decadent alternative to traditional rum balls!

Icing (confectioner's) sugar	1 3/4 cups	425 mL
Vanilla wafer crumbs	1 cup	250 mL
Finely chopped walnuts	1/2 cup	125 mL
Butter, softened	1/4 cup	60 mL
Water	2 tbsp.	30 mL
Rum extract	1/2 tsp.	2 mL
Icing (confectioner's) sugar	1/3 cup	75 mL

Measure first 6 ingredients into large bowl. Mix until stiff dough forms. Roll into balls, using about 1 tbsp. (15 mL) for each.

Roll balls in second amount of icing sugar in small shallow dish until coated. Makes about 24 balls.

1 ball: 93 Calories; 4.2 g Total Fat (1.2 g Mono,1.2 g Poly, 1.5 g Sat); 8 mg Cholesterol; 14 g Carbohydrate; trace Fibre; 1 g Protein; 32 mg Sodium

hazelnut truffles

These rich, bittersweet chocolate treats full of crunchy hazelnuts are a not-too-sugary gift for someone who's already sweet enough!

Brown sugar, packed	1/3 cup	75 mL
Golden corn syrup	3 tbsp.	50 mL
Hard margarine (or butter)	3 tbsp.	50 mL
Cocoa, sifted if lumpy	2 tbsp.	30 mL
Vanilla extract	1/2 tsp.	2 mL
Finely chopped, flaked hazelnuts (filberts), toasted (see Tip, page 64)	1 cup	250 mL
Whole hazelnuts (filberts), skins removed and toasted (see Tip, page 64)	16	16
Finely chopped, flaked hazelnuts (filberts), toasted (see Tip, page 64)	1/4 cup	60 mL

Combine first 5 ingredients in medium heavy saucepan. Heat and stir on medium for about 2 minutes until margarine is melted and sugar is dissolved. Remove from heat.

Add first amount of flaked hazelnuts. Mix well. Roll into balls, using about 1 tbsp. (15 mL) for each.

Push 1 whole hazelnut into centre of each ball. Roll balls to enclose hazelnuts in chocolate mixture.

Roll balls in second amount of flaked hazelnuts in small shallow dish until coated. Makes about 16 truffles.

1 truffle: 117 Calories; 8.9 g Total Fat (6.6 g Mono, 0.9 g Poly, 1 g Sat); 0 mg Cholesterol; 10 g Carbohydrate; 1 g Fibre; 2 g Protein; 33 mg Sodium

kona truffles

To shape these sinfully delicious truffles, it helps to rub a little butter on your hands, or apply some cooking spray, to them.

Semi-sweet chocolate chips	2 cups	500 mL
Can of sweetened condensed milk	11 oz.	300 mL
Chopped walnuts	3/4 cup	175 mL
Vanilla extract	1 tsp.	5 mL
Medium unsweetened coconut, toasted (optional), see Tip, page 64	1 cup	250 mL

Heat chocolate chips in medium heavy saucepan on lowest heat, stirring often, until almost melted. Do not overheat. Remove from heat. Stir until smooth.

Add next 3 ingredients. Stir well. Chill for at least 6 hours or overnight. Roll into 1 inch (2.5 cm) balls.

Roll balls in coconut in small shallow dish until coated. Place on waxed paper-lined baking sheet with sides. Chill. Makes about 48 truffles.

1 truffle: 84 Calories; 5.5 g Total Fat (1.3 g Mono, 0.9 g Poly, 3.0 g Sat); 3 mg Cholesterol; 9 g Carbohydrate; 1 g Fibre; 1 g Protein; 12 mg Sodium

tartufi

Guests will be stumped by the secret ingredient in these fabulous Italian truffles, but they'll keep reaching for more to figure it out. A good-quality dark chocolate is a must. You can substitute 1 tbsp. (15 mL) orange liqueur for the balsamic vinegar. Refrigerate these in an airtight container for up to a week, or in the freezer for up to a month.

Dark chocolate bar, chopped	3 1/2 oz.	100 g
Whipping cream	1/3 cup	75 mL
Balsamic vinegar	2 tsp.	10 mL
Chocolate sprinkles	6 tbsp.	100 mL

Heat chocolate and whipping cream in small heavy saucepan on lowest heat, stirring often, until almost melted. Do not overheat. Remove from heat. Stir until smooth.

Add vinegar. Stir. Chill, uncovered, for about 1 hour, stirring occasionally, until just firm enough to roll into balls. Roll into balls, using about 2 tsp. (10 mL) for each.

Roll balls in chocolate sprinkles in small shallow dish until coated. Place on waxed paper-lined baking sheet with sides. Chill. Makes about 16 truffles.

1 truffle: 62 Calories; 4.5 g Total Fat (1.4 g Mono, 0.1 g Poly, 2.7 g Sat); 7 mg Cholesterol; 6 g Carbohydrate; trace Fibre; 1 g Protein; 5 mg Sodium

jewelled fruit bites

Sparkly sugar and colourful glazed fruit give these confections the look of diamonds and jewels! Freeze in an airtight container for up to a month. To thaw, leave them at room temperature for 30 minutes before serving.

Finely crushed vanilla wafers (about 36 wafers)	1 cup	250 mL
Marsala wine	1/4 cup	60 mL
White chocolate baking squares (1 oz., 28 g, each), chopped	3	3
Finely chopped mixed glazed fruit	1 3/4 cups	425 mL
White sanding (decorating) sugar (see Tip, page 64)	1/2 cup	125 mL

Combine wafer crumbs and wine in medium bowl. Let stand, covered, at room temperature for 1 hour.

Heat chocolate in small heavy saucepan on lowest heat, stirring often, until almost melted. Do not overheat. Remove from heat. Stir until smooth. Add to crumb mixture. Mix well. Chill, uncovered, for about 15 minutes until firm enough to roll into balls. Roll into balls, using about 1 tsp. (5 mL) for each.

Roll balls in glazed fruit in small bowl. Roll balls in sanding sugar in small shallow dish until coated. Makes about 40 balls.

1 ball: 67 Calories; 1.2 g Total Fat (0.4 g Mono, 0.2 g Poly, 0.5 g Sat); 3 mg Cholesterol; 14 g Carbohydrate; trace Fibre; trace Protein; 19 mg Sodium

raspberry turkish jellies

You can substitute any flavour (and colour!) of sweetened powdered drink crystals as a variation. And instead of coating the jellies in granulated sugar, try icing sugar. These store for up to four weeks between layers of waxed paper in an airtight container.

Granulated sugar	1 3/4 cups	425 mL
Water	1 cup	250 mL
Sweetened powdered raspberry drink crystals	1/4 cup	60 mL
Lemon juice	1 tbsp.	15 mL
Envelopes of unflavoured gelatin (1/4 oz., 7 g, each), about 5 tbsp., 75 mL	5	5
Water	3/4 cup	175 mL
Berry sugar	3 tbsp.	50 mL

Combine first 4 ingredients in large saucepan. Bring to a boil on medium. Boil for 3 to 4 minutes, stirring occasionally, until sugar is dissolved.

Sprinkle gelatin over water in small bowl. Let stand for 1 minute. Add to boiling syrup mixture. Heat and stir for about 1 minute until gelatin is dissolved. Reduce heat to medium-low. Simmer, uncovered, for about 40 minutes, without stirring, until mixture reaches soft ball stage (234° to 240°F, 112° to 116°C) on candy thermometer (see Tip, page 64) or until small amount dropped into very cold water forms a soft ball that flattens on its own accord when removed. Dampen 8 x 8 inch (20 x 20 cm) or 9 x 9 inch (22 x 22 cm) pan with cold water. Immediately pour syrup mixture into pan. Let stand, uncovered, at room temperature for at least 24 hours until very firm.

Put berry sugar into small shallow bowl. Coat long, sharp knife with berry sugar. Cut along inside edges of pan. Cut jelly mixture into 4 equal portions, coating knife with more berry sugar before each cut. Pull jelly sections from pan, 1 at a time, and place on berry sugar-coated surface. Sprinkle berry sugar as needed to prevent sticking. Cut jellies into 1 inch (2.5 cm) pieces. Press all sides of jelly pieces into berry sugar until coated. Makes about 80 jellies.

1 jelly: 25 Calories; 0 g Total Fat (0 g Mono, 0 g Poly, 0 g Sat); 0 mg Cholesterol; 6 g Carbohydrate; 0 g Fibre; trace Protein; 1 mg Sodium

ginger chocolate cups

Bold ginger flavour accents creamy milk chocolate. Choose different colours of candy cups for a colourful presentation, or match them to a particular table setting.

Milk chocolate bars (3 1/2 oz., 100 g, each), chopped	4	4
Coarsely chopped crystallized ginger	1 cup	250 mL
Foil (or paper) candy cups (1 1/4 inch, 3 cm, diameter)	30	30
Minced crystallized ginger	1 tbsp.	15 mL

Heat chocolate in medium heavy saucepan on lowest heat, stirring often, until almost melted. Do not overheat. Remove from heat. Stir until smooth.

Add first amount of ginger. Mix well. Spoon into candy cups set in mini-muffin cups.

Sprinkle with second amount of ginger. Chill for about 30 minutes until set. Makes 30 chocolate cups.

1 chocolate cup: 78 Calories; 4.1 g Total Fat (1.3 g Mono, 0.1 g Poly, 2.5 g Sat); 3 mg Cholesterol; 10 g Carbohydrate; trace Fibre; 1 g Protein; 13 mg Sodium

petite pears

These easily sculpted, beautifully coloured little pears with a sweet almond flavour can be made ahead and stored in an airtight container at room temperature for up to a month.

Almond paste, room temperature	3 oz.	85 g
Drops of yellow liquid food colouring	2	2
Cocoa, sifted if lumpy	1/4 tsp.	1 mL
Cocoa, sifted if lumpy, just a pinch		
Pieces of shoestring licorice, any colour (1/4 inch, 6 mm, each)	6	6

Put almond paste into small bowl. Knead in food colouring and first amount of cocoa until colour is even (see Tip, page 64). Roll mixture into 6 inch (15 cm) long log. Cut into 6 equal pieces. Roll pieces into balls. Pinch balls to form pear shape. Flatten bottoms slightly so pears will stand upright.

Lightly brush tops of pears with finger dipped in second amount of cocoa. Insert 1 licorice piece in top of each for stem. Makes 6 pears.

1 pear: 65 Calories; 3.9 g Total Fat (2.5 g Mono, 0.8 g Poly, 0.4 g Sat); 0 mg Cholesterol; 7 g Carbohydrate; 2 g Fibre; 2 g Protein; 2 mg Sodium

almond-stuffed dates

Simple, satisfying and a change from the usual holiday baking. The Medjool date featured in this recipe is considered to be the "King of Dates" due to its large size, soft flesh and extreme sweetness. You can refrigerate these dates in an airtight container for up to a month.

Fresh whole Medjool dates	6	6
Almond paste, cut into 6 equal pieces, room temperature	1 1/2 oz.	43 g
Whole natural almonds, toasted (see Tip, page 64)	6	6

Cut 1 inch (2.5 cm) slit lengthwise in each date. Discard pits.

Roll each piece of almond paste into 3/4 inch (2 cm) long log. Insert 1 log lengthwise into each date. Press 1 almond into centre of almond paste in each. Dates will remain open. Makes 6 stuffed dates.

1 stuffed date: 61 Calories; 2.5 g Total Fat (1.6 g Mono, 0.5 g Poly, 0.2 g Sat); 0 mg Cholesterol; 9 g Carbohydrate; 2 g Fibre; 1 g Protein; 1 mg Sodium

quick marshmallows

Colourful cubes of fluff to brighten a sweets tray. For a more adult version, toast the coconut instead of colouring it. And for a fat-free version, omit the coconut and roll the marshmallows in icing sugar instead.

Envelopes of unflavored gelatin (1/4 oz., 7 g, each), about 3 tbsp., 50 mL	3	3
Water	1 1/2 cups	375 mL
Granulated sugar	2 1/4 cups	550 mL
Vanilla extract	1 tsp.	5 mL
Medium unsweetened coconut	1 cup	250 mL
Drops of blue liquid food colouring	3	3
Drops of green liquid food colouring	3	3
Drops of red liquid food colouring	3	3
Drops of yellow liquid food colouring	3	3

Sprinkle gelatin over water in medium saucepan. Let stand for 1 minute.

Add sugar and vanilla. Heat and stir on medium until gelatin and sugar are dissolved. Remove from heat. Cool until you can almost hold your hand on side of saucepan. Beat on high for 15 to 20 minutes until stiff peaks form. Transfer marshmallow mixture to ungreased 9 x 13 inch (22 x 33 cm) pan. Spread evenly. Chill until firm. Cut into 1 1/4 inch (3 cm) squares.

Divide coconut among 4 small jars. Add 1 colour of food colouring to each jar. Shake well. Spread coconut on waxed paper, 1 colour at a time. Roll marshmallows in coconut. Makes 77 marshmallows.

1 marshmallow: 28 Calories; 0.3 g Total Fat (trace Mono, 0 g Poly, 0.3 g Sat); 0 mg Cholesterol; 6 g Carbohydrate; trace Fibre ; trace Protein; 3 mg Sodium

butter pecan pudding fudge

This simple microwave fudge recipe requires no candy thermometer and is prepared in just a few minutes. Store this soft fudge in the refrigerator for up to a week.

Butter	2 tsp.	10 mL
Chopped pecans	1/2 cup	125 mL
Box of butterscotch pudding powder (not instant), 6-serving size	1	1
Milk	1/3 cup	75 mL
Vanilla extract	1 tsp.	5 mL
Butter	3 tbsp.	50 mL
Icing (confectioner's) sugar	2 1/2 cups	625 mL

Melt first amount of butter in small shallow frying pan on medium. Add pecans. Cook for 3 to 5 minutes, stirring often, until pecans are golden. Set aside.

Whisk next 3 ingredients in large microwave-safe bowl until smooth. Add second amount of butter. Microwave, uncovered, on high (100%) for 1 minute. Whisk until smooth. Microwave on high (100%) for 30 seconds. Whisk. Microwave on high (100%) for 50 to 60 seconds until just beginning to bubble on side of bowl. Do not overcook. Whisk.

Immediately whisk in icing sugar until thickened. Stir in pecan mixture. Line 9 x 5 x 3 inch (22 x 12.5 x 7.5 cm) loaf pan with foil, leaving 1 inch (2.5 cm) overhang on long sides. Grease foil with cooking spray. Press mixture evenly in pan. Chill until firm. Holding foil, remove fudge from pan. Discard foil. Cuts into 40 pieces.

1 piece: 67 Calories; 2.2 g Total Fat (1.0 g Mono, 0.3 g Poly, 0.8 g Sat); 3 mg Cholesterol; 12 g Carbohydrate; trace Fibre; trace Protein; 27 mg Sodium

white chocolate fudge

The joy of this fudge is that it can be served as is, for snow-white contrast on a plate of colourful candies, or it can be drizzled with a little bit of melted chocolate for an extra cocoa hit.

Block of cream cheese, softened	8 oz.	250 g
Icing (confectioner's) sugar	4 cups	1 L
White chocolate baking squares (1 oz., 28 g, each), chopped	12	12
Ground pecans	2/3 cup	150 mL
Vanilla extract	1 1/2 tsp.	7 mL

Put cream cheese into large bowl. Beat in icing sugar, 1 cup (250 mL) at a time, until smooth.

Heat chocolate in large heavy saucepan on lowest heat, stirring often, until chocolate is almost melted. Do not overheat. Remove from heat. Stir until smooth. Add to cream cheese mixture. Stir well.

Add pecans and vanilla. Stir well. Line 8 x 8 inch (20 x 20 cm) pan with foil, leaving 1 inch (2.5 cm) overhang on 2 sides. Grease foil with cooking spray. Spread chocolate mixture evenly in prepared pan. Chill until firm. Holding foil, remove fudge from pan. Discard foil. Cuts into 64 squares.

1 square: 80 Calories; 3.8 g Total Fat (1.5 g Mono, 0.4 g Poly, 3.6 g Sat); 9 mg Cholesterol; 11 g Carbohydrate; trace Fibre; 1 g Protein; 16 mg Sodium

double-decker fudge

A creamy, smooth layer of peanut butter topped by another of chocolate creates an eye-catching treat for a dessert platter.

Granulated sugar	2 1/4 cups	550 mL
Jar of marshmallow creme	7 oz.	198 g
Evaporated milk (or half-and-half cream)	3/4 cup	175 mL
Hard margarine (or butter)	1/4 cup	60 mL
Vanilla extract	1 tsp.	5 mL
Peanut butter chips	1 cup	250 mL
Semi-sweet chocolate chips	1 cup	250 mL

Combine first 4 ingredients in large heavy saucepan. Bring to a rolling boil on medium, stirring often. Boil for 5 minutes, stirring constantly. Remove from heat.

Add vanilla. Stir.

Pour 2 cups (500 mL) marshmallow mixture over peanut butter chips in medium bowl. Stir vigorously until melted. Line 8 x 8 inch (20 x 20 cm) pan with foil, leaving 1 inch (2.5 cm) overhang on 2 sides. Grease foil with cooking spray. Spread peanut butter mixture evenly in prepared pan.

Pour remaining marshmallow mixture over chocolate chips in separate medium bowl. Stir vigorously until melted. Spread over peanut butter layer in pan. Chill until firm. Holding foil, remove fudge from pan. Discard foil. Cuts into 48 pieces.

1 piece: 107 Calories; 3.7 g Total Fat (1.0 g Mono, 0.1 g Poly, 2.1 g Sat); trace Cholesterol; 21 g Carbohydrate; trace Fibre; 2 g Protein; 33 mg Sodium

old-fashioned toffee

The rich, sweet flavour of this traditional toffee makes a lovely gift for someone special.

Brown sugar, packed	1 1/4 cups	300 mL
Can of sweetened condensed milk	11 oz.	300 mL
Corn syrup	1/4 cup	60 mL
Hard margarine (or butter)	1/4 cup	60 mL

Combine all 4 ingredients in medium heavy saucepan. Bring to a boil on medium-low, stirring constantly, until mixture reaches firm ball stage (242° to 248°F, 117° to 120°C) on candy thermometer (see Tip, page 64) or until a small amount dropped into very cold water forms a pliable ball. Spread evenly in well greased 8 x 8 inch (20 x 20 cm) pan. Let stand for 10 minutes. Score top of toffee into 1 inch (2.5 cm) squares using sharp knife. Cool completely. Remove from pan. Break into pieces. Makes about 64 pieces.

1 piece: 47 Calories; 1.3 g Total Fat (0.7 g Mono, 0.1 g Poly, 0.5 g Sat); 2 mg Cholesterol; 9 g Carbohydrate; trace Fibre; trace Protein; 19 mg Sodium

white chocolate popcorn

How can you make caramel-coated popcorn even better? Follow this recipe
for pure decadence.

White chocolate bars (3 1/2 oz., 100 g, each), chopped	3	3
Bag of caramel-coated popcorn and peanuts (about 5 cups, 1.25 L)	7 oz.	200 g
Slivered almonds, toasted (see Tip, page 64)	1/2 cup	125 mL

Heat chocolate in medium heavy saucepan on lowest heat, stirring often, until chocolate is almost melted. Do not overheat. Remove from heat. Stir until smooth.

Spread popcorn on foil-lined baking sheet with sides. Drizzle chocolate over popcorn. Stir. Sprinkle with almonds. Chill until set. Break into bite-sized pieces. Makes about 5 1/2 cups (1.4 L).

1/2 cup (125 mL): 255 Calories; 13 g Total Fat (5.2 g Mono, 1.5 g Poly, 5.3 g Sat); 6 mg Cholesterol; 33 g Carbohydrate; 1 g Fibre; 4 g Protein; 79 mg Sodium

recipe index

topical tips

Candy thermometer test: Test your candy thermometer before each use. Bring water to a boil. Candy thermometer should read 212°F (100°C) at sea level. Adjust recipe temperature up or down based on test results. For example, if your thermometer reads 206°F (97°C), subtract 6°F (3°C) from each temperature called for in recipe.

Keeping hands clear of food colouring: To avoid staining your hands with the food colouring, wear disposable plastic gloves when kneading.

Peeling hazelnuts: To peel hazelnuts, spread toasted nuts on half of tea towel. Fold other half over nuts. Press down and rub vigorously for 1 to 2 minutes, until almost all skins are removed. You may not be able to remove all skins from the hazelnuts, but the outer paper skins should come off.

Sanding (decorating) sugar: Sanding sugar is a coarse decorating sugar that comes in white and various colours and is available at specialty kitchen stores.

Toasting nuts, seeds or coconut: Cooking times will vary for each type of nut—so never toast them together. For small amounts, place ingredient in an ungreased shallow frying pan. Heat on medium for 3 to 5 minutes, stirring often, until golden. For larger amounts, spread ingredient evenly in an ungreased shallow pan. Bake in 350°F (175°C) oven for 5 to 10 minutes, stirring or shaking often, until golden.

Nutrition Information Guidelines

Each recipe is analyzed using the Canadian Nutrient File from Health Canada, which is based on the United States Department of Agriculture (USDA) Nutrient Database.

- If more than one ingredient is listed (such as "butter or hard margarine"), or if a range is given (1–2 tsp., 5–10 mL), only the first ingredient or first amount is analyzed.

- For meat, poultry and fish, the serving size per person is based on the recommended 4 oz. (113 g) uncooked weight (without bone), which is 2–3 oz. (57–85 g) cooked weight (without bone)— approximately the size of a deck of playing cards.

- Milk used is 1% M.F. (milk fat), unless otherwise stated.

- Cooking oil used is canola oil, unless otherwise stated.

- Ingredients indicating "sprinkle," "optional," or "for garnish" are not included in the nutrition information.

- The fat in recipes and combination foods can vary greatly depending on the sources and types of fats used in each specific ingredient. For these reasons, the count of saturated, monounsaturated and polyunsaturated fats may not add up to the total fat content.